A Complete Guide To

Creating Tasty Spaces

By Felicia Lisa Middleton

The Foodie Builder

Designing and Building Food Facilities

Copyright © 2019 by Felicia Lisa Middleton

All rights reserved. This book or any portion thereof may not be reproduced or used in any manner whatsoever without the express written permission of Felicia Lisa Middleton, The Foodie Builder (www.foodiebuilder.com) except for the use of brief quotations in a book review.

Printed in the United States of America
First Printing, 2019
ISBN 978-1-080-00212-2
Poetricia Publishing
PO Box 8963
Collingswood, NJ 08108
www.poetriciapublishing.com

Cover Art by Tiffany Eliza Gray (le.designs@outlook.com)

Ordering Information
www.amazon.com/author/thefoodiebuilder

"Form ever follows function." – Louis Sullivan

A Complete Guide to Creating Tasty Spaces

PREFACE

It all started with a checklist. A Food Facility Checklist that I created early in my entrepreneurial career to cover the process of completing a Food Facility project I found that many clients run into roadblocks - often costly roadblocks - because of their lack of knowledge, their inability, or their unwillingness to follow a process.

When I found that these types of checklists often weren't followed, I decided to expand my checklist to a book. Then I further developed it into a comprehensive workbook that would provide short explanations to help develop a plan and move through each step in the process. While working on various challenging projects, I discovered when, how, and where disconnects occur as the design and build out processes plays out.

Readers and potential restaurateurs can navigate through each step in this guide, with a focus on the important factors that should be considered early in the food facility process.

This workbook does not seek to eliminate problems, but help you understand where challenges may lie, as well as help you develop plans to solve those matters in the most efficient ways possible.

Felicia Middleton
The Foodie Builder

A Complete Guide to Creating Tasty Spaces

FOREWORD

In the 30 plus years that I've been in the restaurant and nightclub industry I have learned the hard way about design, planning and execution of new restaurant design and construction. I have always been skeptical of designers or architects in this fickle and ever-changing field because what looks good on paper many times is a disaster in practice. The Restaurant and Nightclub Business has more dimensions than many will ever understand but it seems that Felicia has done her homework.

"The Foodie Builder's Complete Guide to Creating Tasty Spaces" is a thorough guide to opening a food and beverage location from the ground up, covering very important areas that many would overlook, focused only on the end result. Legal, Zoning, Financial, Health and Wellness, Brand Concept, Service and Design are a few major points that must come together as one in order to achieve success. Felicia has hit on all of these points with simple to understand, clear and visual attention.

Well done and "*Buona Fortuna*!"

Paul Marrone
A Tutti Ristorante Italiano

A Complete Guide to Creating Tasty Spaces

A COMPLETE GUIDE TO CREATING TASTY SPACES

TABLE OF CONTENTS

Preface	5
Foreword	7
Introduction	11

I. CONCEPTUALIZE

Designing Your Tasty Space: Trust The Process	13
The Menu Rules Your Tasty Space	19
Elements Of A Tasty Space	25

II. PLANNING

Finding Your Tasty Space	49
Financing Your Tasty Space	55

III. PROCESS

Building Your Tasty Space	61
What To Expect When Your Tasty Space Is Inspected	69
Permitted To Build; Licensed To Operate Your Tasty Space	73
Examples Of Tasty Spaces	77
Tasty Tips	101
Tasty Terms	103
Tasty Food Facility Checklist	107

Acknowledgements	111
About The Author	113
Other Books By The Author	114
Notes	115

A Complete Guide to Creating Tasty Spaces

INTRODUCTION

For over ten years, Felicia Middleton, *The Foodie Builder*, has developed from a budding entrepreneur to a well-respected, successful, and sought-after designer. As the owner of Urban Aesthetics, a Philadelphia based design and planning firm, Felicia has reached new heights in her career with this important publication. This workbook will help you better understand where challenges may lie, as well as help you develop plans to solve those matters in the most efficient ways possible.

Divided into three sections: Conceptualize, Planning and Process, *A Complete Guide to Creating Tasty Spaces* focuses on a wide variety of topics such as building safety, contractor experience, and building design just to name a few. Felicia is concerned about the usefulness of her publication and has therefore included a variety of checklists, diagrams, and illustrations to help the reader understand key points such as permits, building safety and spending.

Felicia's *A Complete Guide to Creating Tasty Spaces* comes at an appropriate time as Philadelphia has become one of the great foodie cities on the East Coast. In August 2018, *Travel and Leisure* declared Philadelphia to be the best food city on the East Coast right now. As *Salon* reported in May 2019 "Philadelphia has a robust farmer's markets and community supported agriculture groups sustained by the farming community of Pennsylvania and New Jersey. Seasonal, locally grown produce is as big a deal, if not bigger, than it is in Brooklyn."

For food entrepreneurs in and around the Philadelphia region, reading *A Complete Guide to Creating Tasty Spaces* is a critical early step to success. As you create your space, hire the right staff, and design a unique menu, add reading *A Complete Guide to Creating Tasty Spaces* to your list. Doing so will ensure that you prepare accordingly as you navigate the complexities of becoming a food entrepreneur.

Michael Edmondson, Ph.D.
Author of *Success: Theory and Practice*

A Complete Guide to Creating Tasty Spaces

I. CONCEPTUALIZE

Designing Your Tasty Space
Trust the Process

All great design projects are the result of a process. Trusting the process in this guide will ensure that your design project will be completed efficiently and effectively. As you move through this process, you will coordinate and collaborate with experts in the field that will help you accomplish your goal.

Many successful design projects are guided by a team of design professionals that include individuals in the fields of Architecture, Interior Design and several areas of Engineering. Skipping steps in the process translates to poor planning and will result in last minute changes that could lead to costly mistakes.

In the design field, following a Design Process will allow you to manage and complete your projects.

Our Design Process consists of the following phases:

Pre-Design

- Initial Consultation
- Facility Walk Through

- Project Assessment : Type of Facility, Menu, Location, Preliminary Budget
- Scope Planning
- Evaluation of Existing Conditions

Design Development

- Design Concepts
- Concept Modification
- Code Review

Construction Documentation

- Coordination with Consultants
- Working Drawings
- Application of Permit Requirements to Drawings

Construction Phase

- Permits Issued
- Construction / Build-out

Inspection Phase

- Punch List
- Inspections
- Certificates Of Occupancy

The main goal of the designer is to plan and manage your project (with your end goal in mind) while adhering to building codes and design standards. Design professionals often coordinate with others in overlapping professions in order to achieve that goal.

With most restaurant projects, you will need an Architectural professional with a knowledge of Back of House and Commercial Kitchens, Health Department requirements and Commercial Building Code applications. In order to handle the changes in electrical, plumbing, exhaust and air flow requirements, you will likely need a Mechanical Engineer. You may also need an Interior Designer skilled in material selection and styles who will be helpful in expressing your brand style and creating your design and feel for the Front Of House. If there are any structural changes, a Structural Engineer will be required to ensure that your building will be safe structurally.

Design projects can be challenging, but the goal is to follow the process in order to create the look and function within a space. Following the process also allows you to solve problems sooner rather than later.

You can create a new space that fits your needs with an existing building or with new construction. However, keep in mind that you will be governed by laws and standards that are created in order to protect and ensure the health, safety and welfare of the public. With food facilities in particular, strict requirements are maintained for food safety and food handling needs.

Through The Process

- Pre-Design Phase:
- Design Development Phase:
- Construction Document Phase:
    -Permit Review:
- Construction Phase:
- Inspection Phases:

DESIGN PROCESS

DEFINE
Pre-Design Phase
Initial Consultation
Site Evaluation

CREATE
Design Development Phase
Design Concepts
Concept Modification

PROTOTYPE
Construction Documentation Phase
Coordination with Consultants

BUILD
Permits Issued
Construction Phase

ANALYZE
Inspections
Certificate Of Occupancy

Who is your target customer?

What is your ideal style?

What are your brand colors?

The Menu Rules Your Tasty Spaces

With Yolanda Lockhart- Davis
Chef and Food Service Consultant
Owner of Salt Pepper and Soul LLC

Imagine finally getting a reservation at one of the hottest, most prestigious, restaurants in the city. After deciding on your finest attire, you arrive at the restaurant, and are greeted by a beautifully knowledgeable server who hands you a MENU that will be the starting point for your entire gourmet dining experience.

Every Chef who dreams of opening his or her own restaurant has visions of serving their food to adoring guests night after night and planning their MENU in deliciously descriptive detail.

For the restaurant owner, the MENU is the central point of their existence. Everything that happens in the dining room, in the kitchen, and in the back office is driven by the MENU as the restaurant's primary source of revenue.

Two of the biggest reasons why otherwise popular restaurants close is (1) failure to manage food costs, and (2) failure to ensure that menu pricing will cover expenses (*for Food & Beverage components, Labor, and Rent/Mortgage/Utilities*) while consistently generating a profit every month.

According to *Chef and Food Service Consultant Yolanda Lockhart- Davis*, the MENU is "the center of the plate", and the most essential element of a restaurant's overall budget and business plan.

Famed architect Louis Sullivan once coined the phrase "Form Follows Function". This philosophy has been the source of great debate in the world of architecture. However, in Food Facility Design, this philosophy rules.

The Foodie Builder routinely encourages restaurant clients to begin the planning phase of the restaurant's design process by planning the MENU. The Menu will determine what equipment is needed in the kitchen, the kitchen size, the number of staff needed for food preparation & service, and the proper workflow to ensure that food is prepared and served to the guest as efficiently as possible.

The MENU also drives the mechanical, plumbing, utility and electrical design. For example, if your menu features steamed and/or fried foods, the kitchen may require the following at a minimum:

- Commercial Deep Fryers (Gas-Powered)
- Commercial Steamers (Gas or Electric, with a Dedicated Water Line and Water Filtration)
- 6-10 Burner Stove (Gas or Electric)
- Exhaust Hood (Electric, with corresponding ductwork leading to the building exterior)
- Refrigerator and/or Freezer (Electric)

Everyone knows that "location, location, location" can be a critical component to a restaurant's success, but the MENU is so important that it should be established even BEFORE selecting your location. First-time restaurant owners don't always realize that the building you choose needs to meet your plumbing, utility and electrical requirements in order to support your kitchen equipment. Adding these elements or having to make significant structural changes to an existing facility can be costly and take a large chunk out of your budget before the first meal is ever prepared or served.

In our experience, the MENU is often one of the last items on the mind of the restaurateur, especially if the restauranteur is not a Chef. In order to set your restaurant up for success, make sure planning your MENU is at the forefront of the restaurant design process to establish your equipment list, facility requirements, labor requirements, and overall restaurant budget.

Yolanda Lockhart-Davis is a Nutrition-Focused Chef & Food Service Consultant with expertise in Menu Analysis & Development; Consolidated Ordering & Cost Control; Food Costing & Quality Assurance; Food Safety Documentation; Food Safety Protocol Implementation; POS System Configuration; Production Staffing; Project Management; Policy & Procedure Documentation; and Vendor Management.

Do you have a menu planned?

What are your menu "must haves"?

What may be on your expanded menu?

The Menu Rules Your Tasty Space

Elements Of A Tasty Space

Several basic yet important items make up a Tasty Space. The items are not limited to one area, and some items can be extremely costly. There are items that are required for you to be able to open your facility.

In the Front of House, the main items will include the Service Counter, Point Of Sales Area, Bar; Seating and Dining Area; Hostess and Pick Up Areas. In the Back of House, the items include your Food Preparation Equipment; Cooking Equipment and Cleaning and Storage spaces and Equipment.

The following pages reflect important elements located in the Back Of House, and two examples of a restaurant's Front of House. Most often, in restaurants with bars and cafes, equipment is included in both the Back of House and the Front of House. As you review the elements selected in this chapter, keep in mind there many other equipment items that may also be required for your facility.

WORK TABLE

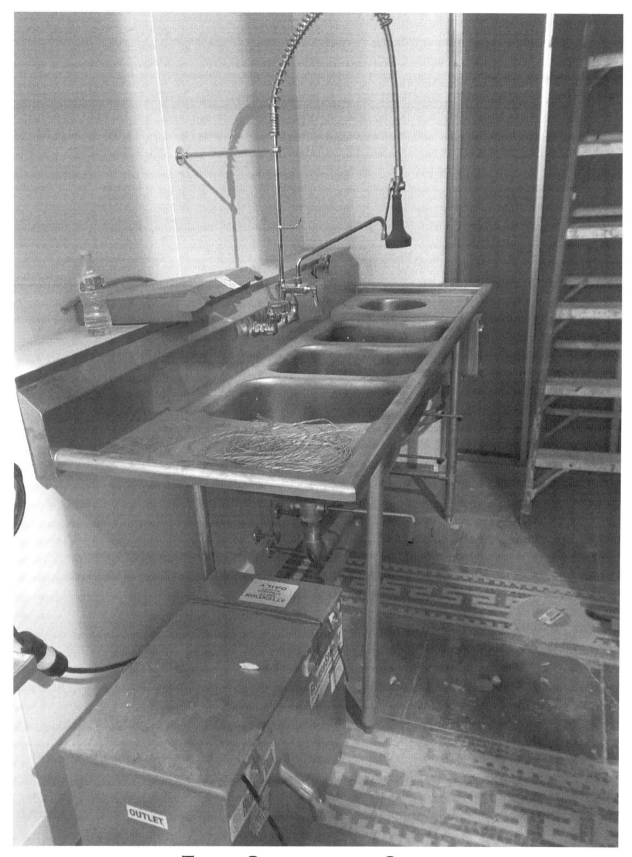

THREE COMPARTMENT SINK

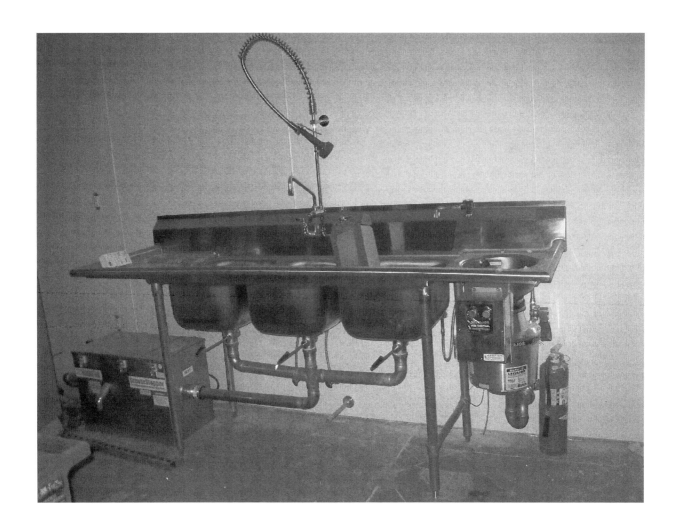

THREE COMPARTMENT SINK

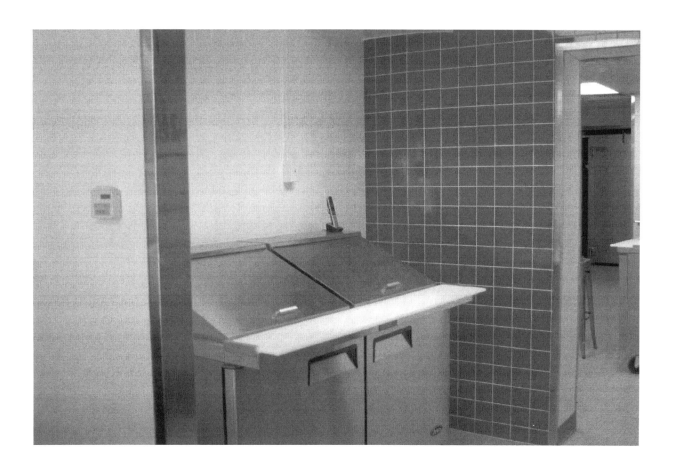

SANDWICH TABLE

SANDWICH TABLE AND OVERHEAD SHELVING

REACH IN REFRIGERATOR

REACH IN FREEZER

PIZZA OVEN

HAND SINK

Hand Sink

GREASE TRAP

GAS RANGE

FRONT OF HOUSE

FRONT OF HOUSE

FRONT OF HOUSE

FLOOR SINK

FIRE SUPPRESSION SYSTEM

Exhaust Hood

Exhaust Hood

CONVENTION OVEN

EQUIPMENT LIST

ITEM	QTY	MANUFACTURER	REMARKS

How much dry storage will you need?

How much cold storage will you need?

How much frozen storage will you need?

Elements of a Tasty Space

II. PLANNING

Finding Your Tasty Space

When you begin your search for your Tasty Space, one of the first things to consider should be the Real Estate Professional that you will choose. For restaurants, cafes and food service facilities, a Real Estate Professional with a commercial background is best for you. There is a difference in the knowledge of the market between a Commercial Real Estate Professional and a Residential Real Estate Professional. Commercial Real Estate Professionals are skilled at helping consumers choose the right Tasty Space that meets their needs in the ideal location. Commercial Real Estate Professionals also help individuals find the Tasty Property that they will need within their budget and pre-approved financial limits.

Suggestion: Research and interview Commercial Real Estate Professionals who can help you locate your Tasty Space. Make a list of 3 - 5 that you want to talk with. After speaking with each one, choose the one with a knowledge of the area where you wish to open. Make sure they also have a knowledge of Zoning. Later in this chapter you will understand why a knowledge of Zoning is imperative.

When searching for a building, you will want to consider your needs for your business goals, design and utilities. Restaurant equipment draws a large amount of electricity, water and other utilities. It's important to be sure that the building can accommodate all of your needs. You may want to consider taking the designer of your Back of House area and your General Contractor with you when looking for buildings that you are interested in fitting out for your business.

Your equipment list will be a factor in the building that you choose. The size, layout, and utilities needed are also factors. For example, if your cooking requires an exhaust hood, your building will need to have an ideal location for the hood and the ductwork run for the hood. Mixed use buildings often pose challenges for ductwork because of the run of the ductwork. Code may dictate the run of the ductwork on the exterior of the building as well as the interior. Plumbing, floor sinks, and drains also affect the building's structure because of the run of the drain lines.

If you choose to build new construction, your main concern will be that the area where you plan to build has all of the utility services that you need. Consider that some areas and some new construction does not supply natural gas. Also consider that the waste lines may not accommodate your needs and you may need to have utility work done on the building's exterior in order to meet your needs. Taking a General Contractor experienced in fitting out restaurants or commercial spaces on your building search will help you in choosing the right building. Later we will discuss in detail the importance of choosing the right contractor.

One of the most important factors in choosing the right location, whether you build or renovate, is Zoning. In the majority of municipalities in the United States, areas are divided into Zoning Designations such as Residential, Light Commercial, Industrial, etc. Zoning also governs use and occupancy requirements, building heights, area coverage, and signage. Zoning can be confusing because people often think that if a building is Zoned commercial, any commercial use is allowed. Zoning may be more detailed, classifying particular uses to a specific Zoning Designation. For example, in Philadelphia, restaurants have more than one Zoning Use, depending on whether food is eaten on location or taken out.

If you choose a building where the Use for your business will not be allowed, many municipalities will allow you to appeal before their local Zoning Board. There is no guarantee that you will win the decision and Zoning Board decisions can take time and adds more steps in the process of opening your restaurant. The best scenario is to purchase or rent an existing restaurant and renovate the space or follow procedures that will help you make sure you choose a building meets your needs.

TASTY LOCATION PLANNER

POTENTIAL REAL ESTATE AGENTS

_____

_____

_____

_____

NOTES

PROPOSED LOCATIONS

_____

_____

_____

_____

Where is your desired location?

What would you like in the vicinity?

What is your overall desired size?

Financing Your Tasty Space

Financing Your Tasty Space

Contribution By Dr. Renaldo Epps
Consulting Associates, LLC

One of the most important factors in planning and building food facilities is having a sound financial plan. There is too much risk involved with the building, fit-out, and operation of a restaurant to start out without a sound financial plan. Your financial plan should include a Spending Limit; Budget; Funding Sources; Projected Profits and any possible financial risks that may affect your profitability.

To be able to successfully plan out the financials of your project and business operations, first you need to have the ability to understand how money works-become financially literate. Financial literacy is the study of how someone manages to make or earn money, how that person manages it, how he/she invests it and how that person donates it to help others.

Budget

Begin the financial planning of your Tasty Space with a budget and a spending limit. Your spending limit will determine how much you can or want to spend on your project. As you gather information regarding costs, you can list the expenses to determine if your spending limit is realistic or if you may need to obtain additional funding or change the scale of your project.

To create a budget you will need to know your fixed and flexible expenses. These expenses should be listed in detail. The following are examples of expenses that can be listed in a budget.

- Initial Expenses

  A large part of your initial expenses will include the purchase of restaurant equipment. Often, the most expensive piece of equipment will be your exhaust hood. Other expensive pieces may include the dish machine.

- For many restaurant construction build-outs, the largest expenses will be the electrical and plumbing work. In addition to contractor fees and materials for construction, other important costs to consider for your building project are administrative costs and professional fees, such as fees for licenses, permits, and the fees associated with Design Professionals and Engineers.

- Fixed Costs remain constant over a period of time.

  (Rent is an example of a fixed cost.)

- Flexible Costs are costs that vary over time.

  (Travel is an example of a flexible cost.)

- Contingencies should be in your budget in preparation for the unknown.

Funding Sources

Multiple sources are available to help you fund your tasty space. You can obtain funding from Investors, Savings, Personal Financing, Business Financing, Crowd Funding, profits from sales and various other sources. The important factor is to have a dependable funding source that can cover the expenses in your budget.

Credit

If you are seeking to secure financing for your tasty space, you will need to have sound credit. It is very crucial that you keep a good credit score. The information on a consumer's credit card report can be analyzed by the company to decide whether to extend credit to that customer. It is good if your credit history is clear of any bankruptcy or scam charges. Any negative charge on your credit card can stay for seven years, while bankruptcy charges could remain on your credit report for ten years.

It is crucial that you know how to spot any wrong entry in your credit report. To improve your repair your credit score, you also need to understand how it is determined.

The components that affect your score are payment history, the amount you owe, any new credit, length of credit history, and the type of credit you use.

Most people in the United States are unaware that they can improve their credit score themselves without any extra help.

Improve your credit score by following these simple techniques:
- Pay your bills on time.
- Read your credit report regularly and carefully.
- Make sure all activities listed was done by you or under your direct supervision.
- Immediately report any errors you spot and get it corrected.
- Be cautious of online fraud and identity theft, keep your personal information safe.
- Report to Federal Trade Commission immediately if required.

Insurance

Your financial plan should include ways to mitigate risks and ways to cover unexpected expenses. Insurance is a necessary item that should be included in your expenses. Business insurance will serve to protect the business owner, business, and in certain cases even the employees. You will need insurance to protect you and your business from potential loss. The protection could come as a supplement to income lost or in the form of financial aid to repair a business after a disaster.

If a small business has employees, then by law the employer must purchase certain types of insurance, such as workers' compensation insurance, which protects your company from lawsuits and provides financial compensation to employees injured on the job. Starting and running any business can be an expensive venture, and purchasing insurance adds more to the list.

Every business owner should take steps to ensure that they get the most for their money and also save whenever possible. Most standard policies might adequately cover some businesses, but certain industries benefit from specialty or additional business insurance coverage.

Financial Team

To successfully plan for the financing of your tasty space you should build a sound financial team. The financial team is one of the most important aspects of building a healthy business. Without a healthy financial team you can delay the success of your business. Your team should include trusted individuals that can help you create a plan to accomplish your goals.

Your financial team should include an accountant, a bookkeeper, a payroll service, a financial advisor, a business attorney, and a tax adviser.

Dr. Renaldo Octavius Epps is the Founder of Epps Consulting Associates, LLC, Chief Experience Officer of a Paralegal Firm in Wilmington, DE, and a member of the American Bar Association. He is also certified as an Identity Theft Risk Management Specialist from the Institute of Fraud Risk Management.

Sample Budget Worksheet

Account	Amount	Explanation
Administrative Fees		
Professional Fees		
Design Fees		
Financial Professional Fees		
Permit Fees		
Total Administrative Fees		
Construction Fees		
Materials		
Construction		
Finishes		
Total Construction Fees		
Equipment Fees		
Total Equipment Fees		

What is your maximum spending limit?

Have you prepared a budget?

What have you included in your budget?

III. PROCESS

Building Your Tasty Space

Many important factors should be considered when constructing your Tasty Space however I consider the two most important factors to be the selection of your Contractor and obtaining all proper permits. I cannot stress enough how important these two factors will be for a successful construction project. I have witnessed projects delayed or halted, faulty construction, owners fined and the loss of large sums of money due to mistakes made in choosing a contractor and neglecting the permit process.

Make sure that all necessary permits are filed and pulled before you begin work. Never do work that requires a permit before the permit is issued. Working without required permits is a violation of the law and violators may be subject to fines, lawsuits or imprisonment. If you begin construction without the required permits, you will not know if the work is done properly or if it will be approved. Finally, some municipalities require that you are approved for the proper permits before you can legally open.

Suggestions:
- Be in charge of your project
- Demand a copy of all permits (If the contractor does not provide them, halt construction)
- Display permits prominently
- Demand a copy of the approved permit drawings (with approved stamp)
- Keep a copy onsite

Consider hiring a project manager when building out your space. A project manager is a third-party professional who will help you successfully navigate through the design and construction process. The project manager can help you with in several ways, such as managing schedules, managing tasks, and ensuring that the designs are followed properly, and no shortcuts are taken. The project manager can also help you maintain budgets and select the right consultants and contractors.

When selecting your Construction workers, you will need more than one contractor. A General Contractor is licensed to do building work including carpentry, building of walls and structures, repairs and cosmetics. General Contractors are often allowed to connect some plumbing or electrical fixtures with but with limitations and they cannot install all new lines or equipment.

The General Contractor can hire an electrician or Plumber as subcontractors to complete the installation of necessary lines, drains, panels and fixtures. When you hire your contractors, ensure that they are professional and experienced in restaurant construction. Verify that their license and insurance is valid, that their name is on the permits and that their sub-contractors are legitimate as well. I have included a Contractors Checklist to help you in your search and verification of your contractor. I suggest that you compare 3-5 Contractors.

Suggestions:
- Be in charge of your project and/or actively engaged in your project
- Make sure the contractors can read construction documents
- Check their references
- Look at their online reputation
- Review photos of their previous jobs

During construction, contractors should maintain a clean and safe environment. Contractors are required by law to pull required permits and build as the code requires.

You may wonder how you can ensure that they build as code requires. The best way after following all of the suggestions is to have them pull permits and the Inspector will check and verify that their work is done properly.

Restaurant build-outs can be challenging, and coordination is a key factor. After overall construction is done, the contractor or project manager has to coordinate equipment installation, connections and inspection. In addition, coordination of Plumbing, Electric and Ventilation can vary according to equipment delivery and installation.

foodie BUILDER Contractor Checklist

Name of Contractor #1_____

Company:_____

Website:_____Email:_____Phone #:_____

Name of Contractor #2_____

Company:_____

Website:_____Email:_____Phone #:_____

Name of Contractor #3_____

Company:_____

Website:_____Email:_____Phone #:_____

❶ ❷ ❸

Visual proof of Contractor License

Visual proof of Insurance/Bond

Visual proof of Workman's Comp Coverage

Customer References (3-5)

Trade References (Plumber, Electrician, etc.)

Checked Online Reputation (BBB, Angie's List)

Contractor is OSHA 30 Certified

Contractor has a website

Contractor is accessible via multiple forms
of communication (phone, cell, email)

Visual proof of similar project work

Contractor can read/understand construction drawings

Contractor Checklist

Contractor provides Design Services

Contractor understands project requirements

Permit process explained in detail by Contractor

Contractor provides additional services

Detailed, itemized bid submitted

The bid separates labor and materials

Projected start and finish dates indicated

Contractor offers warranties

Contractor will be onsite to supervise crew and subcontractors

Will contractor be working on other projects simultaneously with this project?

The contractor was easy to talk to

The contractor was businesslike and professional

Comfort level (Scale of 1-5; 1 lowest)

 # Contractor Checklist

Name of Contractor #4_____
Company:_____
Website:_____Email:_____Phone #:_____
Name of Contractor #5_____
Company:_____
Website:_____Email:_____Phone #:_____

Visual proof of Contractor License

Visual proof of Insurance/Bond

Visual proof of Workman's Comp Coverage

Customer References (3-5)

Trade References (Plumber, Electrician, etc.)

Checked Online Reputation (BBB, Angie's List)

Contractor is OSHA 30 Certified

Contractor has a website

Contractor is accessible via multiple forms of communication (phone, cell, email)

Visual proof of similar project work

Contractor can read/understand construction drawings

Contractor Checklist

Contractor provides Design Services

Contractor understands project requirements

Permit process explained in detail by Contractor

Contractor provides additional services

Detailed, itemized bid submitted

The bid separates labor and materials

Projected start and finish dates indicated

Contractor offers warranties

Contractor will be onsite to supervise crew and subcontractors

Will contractor be working on other projects simultaneously with this project?

The contractor was easy to talk to

The contractor was businesslike and professional

Comfort level (Scale of 1-5; 1 lowest)

Building Your Tasty Space

What to Expect

When Your Tasty Space is Inspected

Contributions from Lamar Smith

Licensed Health Inspector and Restaurant Owner

Food Service Facilities and Food Manufacturing Facilities are subject to inspections before they open and at times, periodic inspections. In general, the facility should always be Inspector expectant. Initially, several Inspectors may check your space, including the Building, Fire and Health Inspectors, in order to ensure that it has been built or renovated correctly and that it meets the guidelines of the Department Of Health.

The Building Inspectors will check the Building, Electrical and Plumbing work. In many areas, there will be a Pre-Inspection so that the contractor can do a walkthrough and discuss the job with the Building Inspector. The Fire Inspector will check the Fire Protection and Suppression Systems and the Health Inspector checks the overall space, to ensure the safety of the food and food preparation areas.

In preparation for the inspections, all approved, stamped plans should be on site. The space must be free of building debris and the work should be completed. The Inspector, especially the Health Inspector, may ask questions that must be answered correctly. At times, the Inspector may make recommendations that should be done, and they may issue a conditional approval. They can also choose to fail you if the work is not done properly, according to the plans or according to code. At times, the Inspector will require amendments to the plans or the work that is done, if it does not match the plans. All Inspections are done to ensure that the space has been built according to the approved plans and that General Contractor has followed the local, state and the International Building Code. In addition, Health inspections are based on local, state, and federal public health codes. Eating and drinking establishments are normally inspected twice a year, depending on the risk levels.

A Health Inspector's job is to protect the public health of each citizen and to educate the businesses about food safety and sanitation. Once an Inspector enters a facility, he or she may introduce themselves to an employee, business owner, general manager, or supervisor and show proof of identification. Once the introduction is established then the inspection can begin. Once the establishment is open, an Inspector may visit and request service without an introduction, to ensure that proper cleaning, food handling and safety measures are followed.

As a Health Inspector and Consultant I take the approach of multi-tasking during inspections. I always wash my hands and dry them with paper towels. I use gloves while I am inspecting a facility and change them as needed during an audit. During an audit, temperature checks for all cooling units are recorded and cooking and hot holding temperatures are recorded during audits. I observe staff to see if they are washing hands and changing gloves during different tasks. I check all inventory dry goods, dry storage, chemical and utility closets.

Sanitation is a major role in the operational aspects of any eating and drinking facility. Most facilities use a three basin sink for washing, rinsing, and sanitizing. In addition some facilities use chemical based dish machines or heated dish machines to sanitize equipment. Facilities are required to separately store cleaning chemicals including Chlorine, Qac, or Iodine and supply test strips for the cleaning equipment measured in parts per million. The Inspector will ask to see the storage location and will verify that the proper chemicals and test strips are on site.

The Health Inspector will ask a series of questions regarding food handling. The questions must be answered correctly as they often pertain to food handling procedures and proper food handling is critical in an eating or drinking establishment. The questions are asked of the ServeSafe Certified individual on staff. There must be someone who works fulltime in a facility who is ServSafe Certified. This individual is responsible for teaching others about food safety and sanitation.

A health inspector's job is to protect the public health of each citizen. Also, another major duty of a health inspector is to educate the businesses about food safety and sanitation. Once a health inspector enters a facility, he or she must introduce themselves to an employee, business owner, general manager, or supervisor and show proof of identification. Once this introduction is established then the inspection can begin. Paperwork will play a major role for most health inspections, as well as audits. Each facility must have current business licenses, and all required must be posted in public view. The exterior of the facility is also inspected to ensure that all dumpsters are closed, to prevent attraction from vermin, rodents, and insects.

The time when your facility is inspected can be very stressful. The goal is to make sure that all required work is done and done correctly. Your facility should be "operation ready", with all equipment connected and operable; all signs should be in place and all paperwork, including the approved plans, should be on site. Scheduling a "Pre-Inspection Walk-through" can also help you be prepared for and inspection. After all the work is done, have your designer or project manager walk through with the plans and check everything. Make notes of any items that should be addressed and make all necessary corrections. Being prepared in advance is best in order to have a smooth inspection experience

Lamar Smith is an Author, Entrepreneur, Environmental Health Specialist and the owner Dreams Ice Cream Factory in Glenside, PA. Lamar has over a decade of experience with the Montgomery County Board of Health.

Permitted to Build

Licensed To Operate Your Tasty Space

Opening a food facility requires following a list of regulations and obtaining multiple permits and licenses to legally open and operate. Many regulations govern construction, operations and individuals. Often, several permits are required before construction can begin and typically the project is governed by more than one regulatory agency including your local Zoning Department Building Department and Health Department. At times, even more agencies will regulate your project including Historical Planning and the Arts Commission (if applicable for your location or building). Some agencies are Prerequisites to your Zoning and Building Departments and their approval is required in advance.

Ultimately, no building, altering or major repairs are allowed without a permit. This law governs most municipalities, When no prerequisites are required, typically the Zoning Permit is required first.

Zoning governs how a space will be used. Some municipalities categorized uses for food facilities, for example Eat-in and/or Take Out. (Note: although a building is zoned commercial, this does not necessarily mean the use that you desire is allowed.)

Zoning also governs changes in height, changes in square footage, signage, exterior seating, and building footprint.

Building Permits are issued to allow you to make physical alterations to the space. Building Permits govern how a space is built, altered, renovated or repaired and is governed by local, state and the International Building Codes. When alterations are being made to the space, submitting a set of construction drawings will likely be required to have the work approved. The municipality will review the manner in which you plan to modify the space to ensure that you meet the building code requirements. Some municipalities require a building permit for a Certificate of Occupancy, even when there is no work done on the space.

Additional permits are often required to govern the manner in which the trades (plumbers and electricians) will make their modifications and connections. Plumbing permits govern the plumbing and gas fixtures and lines that will be installed. Plumbing permits are typically obtained via plans created by a Mechanical Engineer or Draftsman and can only be obtained via a licensed plumber.

Electrical permits govern the manner in which the electrical lines, panels, loads and fixtures are installed within a structure. Electrical permits are typically obtained via plans created by a Mechanical Engineer or Draftsman and can only be obtained via a licensed electrician.

Mechanical permits govern air flow and mechanical equipment within a facility including Exhaust Hoods, Fans and Heating, Ventilation and Air Conditioning. A mechanical permit is typically obtained with plans prepared by a Mechanical Engineer.

Additional permits may be needed to install fire suppression systems; fire alarm systems and sprinklers. These permits are typically obtained with plans prepared by a Mechanical Engineer.

In addition to permits, licenses are required to operate your food facility and also some equipment within your space. These licenses may include Food Handling Licenses, Scales Licenses and a Business License.

Examples Of Tasty Spaces

Tasty Spaces are well designed and functional food facilities and food areas. The Foodie Builder specializes in designing, planning and building Tasty Spaces.

The following Tasty Spaces include collaborations as well as projects fully designed and planned Felicia Middleton, The Foodie Builder, owner of Urban Aesthetics.

The spaces were projects of Urban Aesthetics between 2010 and 2018. The Foodie Builder's work includes but is not limited to chain restaurants, independent restaurants, franchises, food and cafe accessory areas and spaces in food halls. These Tasty Spaces are located throughout the Philadelphia area.

Examples of Tasty Spaces

Rosa's Fresh Pizza, the ultimate in "Pay It Forward",
helped feed hundreds of thousands of homeless people
in Philadelphia from 2013 through 2019.
Felicia Middleton
The Foodie Builder

Rosa's Fresh Pizza

Rosa's Fresh Pizza

Barry's Buns, a tasty space by the Foodie Builder, located in the Bourse Food Hall in Philadelphia offers tasty baked goods and coffee. Owned and operated by Joel Singer.
Felicia Middleton
The Foodie Builder

Barry's Buns

Tropical Smoothie Cafe, a tasty design-build space by the Foodie Builder, built in 2014, located on Temple University's Campus in Philadelphia, offers healthy fast food and smoothie's.
Felicia Middleton
The Foodie Builder

Examples of Tasty Spaces

Tropical Smoothie Cafe

Tropical Smoothie Cafe

Kari's Tea Bar, a tasty design-build project by the Foodie Builder and BDFS Group, Inc., located at the Bourse Food Hall in Philadelphia, offers original teas blended by PureBlend Tea, its founding company owned by Kari D'eandra.
Felicia Middleton
The Foodie Builder

Kari's Tea Bar

Examples of Tasty Spaces

Bronze Table, a tasty space located in the Bourse Food Hall in Philadelphia offers tasty Italian food. Owned and operated by Joseph D'Andrea.
Felicia Middleton
The Foodie Builder

Bronze Table

Bronze Table

Grub House, a tasty space by the Foodie Builder, located in the Bourse Food Hall in Philadelphia offers tasty breakfast, lunch and coffee. Owned and operated by James Lord.
Felicia Middleton
The Foodie Builder

Grocery and Food Facility, a tasty space located in
the Bourse Food Hall in Philadelphia.
Felicia Middleton
The Foodie Builder

Grocery and Food Facility

Examples of Tasty Spaces

Grocery and Food Facility

Chaat and Chai, a tasty space located in the Bourse Food Hall in Philadelphia offers tasty Indian Food and Chai.
Felicia Middleton
The Foodie Builder

Flow State Coffee Bar, a tasty space by the Foodie Builder, located in the Frankford section of Philadelphia offers tasty pastries, coffee and gelato.
Felicia Middleton
The Foodie Builder

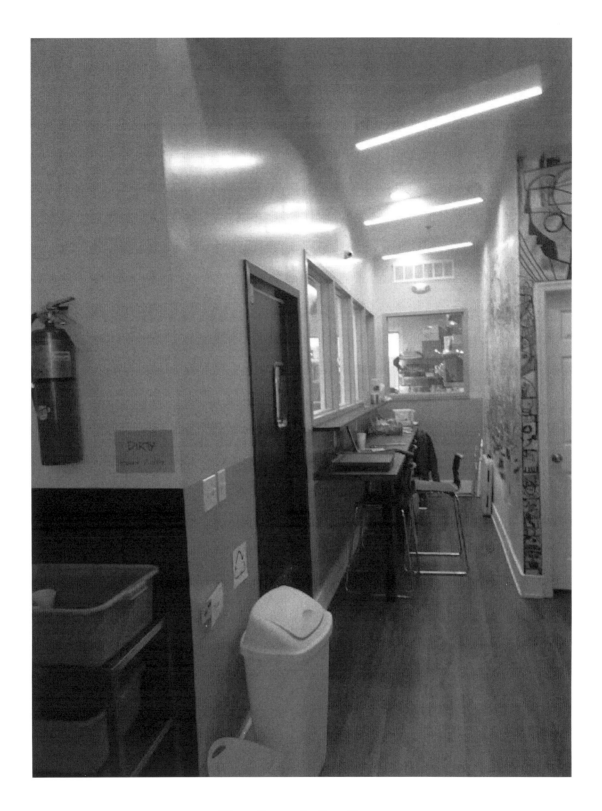

Flow State Coffee Bar

Get Fried, a tasty design-build space by the Foodie Builder, located in The Bourse Food Hall in Philadelphia, offers tasty fries and appetizers.
Felicia Middleton
The Foodie Builder

The Palm Restaurant
A Tasty Space Designed by The Foodie Builder and Studio Torres

The Palm Restaurant
A Tasty Space Designed by The Foodie Builder and Studio Torres

Tasty Tips

Practice building safety.

Hire contractors experienced in building restaurants or commercial facilities.

Seek out your Design Professional early.

Never build without all proper permits.

Market your restaurant before opening.

Verify Zoning and allowed Use for the building.

Research common startup, building and administrative costs.

Create a reasonable spending plan.

Check for violations, building and landlord history.

Verify all requirements before you venture into the project.

Hire trusted professionals.

Project should be planned thoroughly.

Contractor should follow Building Plans.

Contractors do not design; they follow the Design Professional's plans.

Create your menu first.

Hire a Real Estate Professional experienced in commercial buildings.

Consider choosing a building that accommodates your utility needs.

Tasty Terms

Equipment Plan - A part of a full drawing set, displays the equipment layout, referenced by a schedule that lists the manufacturer's information, quantity and other details.

Plumbing Plan - A part of a full drawing set, displays a layout of the plumbing related fixtures and includes the lines and connections. More detailed Plumbing Plans can be included in the Mechanical Plans.

Electrical Plan- A part of a full drawing set, displays a layout of the plumbing related fixtures and includes the lines and connections. More detailed Plumbing Plans can be included in the Mechanical Plans.

Mechanical Engineering Plans - Mechanical, Electrical, Plumbing plans, details and notes prepared by a mechanical designer or engineer.

Shop Drawings - Drawings from a supplier created specifically for fabricated equipment, furniture or custom parts.

Floor Sink - A floor drain, raised above the floor to capture water from an indirectly connected sink.

Tasty Space - A well designed food facility, typically a space designed by the Foodie Builder.

Construction Documentation - This phase produces a set of drawings that include all pertinent information required for the contractor to price and build the project.

Design Development Phase - Further development of the initial design concepts into working documents, coordinating information from a preliminary code review.

Building Permit Drawings - Working Construction Drawings prepared for permit approval.

Pre-Design Phase - the first phase of the design process.

Project Management - Initiating, planning, executing, controlling, and closing the work of a team to achieve the specific goals of the project.

Trades - Referring to construction trades including electricians, carpenters, plumbers, welders, heavy equipment operators and painters, etc.

Warewashing - Area of the Commercial Kitchen where you wash, rinse and sanitize your utensils, and wares needed to prepare and cook food.

Hand Sink - A sink specifically for washing hands only.

Prep Sink - A sink that has a use specifically for washing food that in the preparation process.

Utility Sink - A deep, wide sink used for facility cleaning and dumping of cleaning chemicals grey water.

Warewashing Sink - a sink that has a use specifically for separately washing, rinsing and sanitizing food prep utensils, bowls, etc.

Make Up Air - Fresh air brought in through the exhaust hood to make up for the hot air pulled out by the exhaust.

Cook Line - The row of equipment where food is cooked.

Food Facility - A space designated for the preparing, packaging, storing and consumption of food and beverages.

Back of House - Where food is prepared and stored, includes the commercial kitchen.

Front Of House - Dining or customer space where food is received and consumed.

Food Service Equipment - Sometimes cringingly referred to as "appliances", restaurant equipment refers to the back of house and front of house machines and devices used to store and prepare food and beverages.

National Sanitation Foundation (NSF) - An independent organization that tests and certifies the sanitation and safety of food equipment and supplies.

ServeSafe - An organization that educates and certifies individuals about food handling, preparation and safety.

Tasty Terms

Tasty Food Service Facility Checklist

ADDRESS:

Construction Type:

Square Footage:

Current Zoning:

Seating:

Plans:

- ❏ Site Plan
- ❏ Existing Plan
- ❏ Proposed Plan
- ❏ Equipment Plan and Schedule
- ❏ MEP's
- ❏ Details
- ❏ Elevations:

    Interior

    Exterior

Plans Approval:

- ❏ Building Permit
- ❏ Zoning Permit – Use Change
- ❏ Sign Permit
- ❏ Zoning Special Exception
- ❏ Health Department Approval
- ❏ Historical Committee Approval
- ❏ Arts Commission Approval
- ❏ Streets Department Approval

Occupancy Classification:

- ❏ Group A -
- ❏ Group B -

Occupancy Count:

- ❏ Group A
- ❏ Group B (If Applicable)

Fire Alarm System:

- ❏ Note System
- ❏ Hood Fire Suppression

Accessibility:

- ❏ Ramp (if required)
- ❏ Restroom(s)

Electrical:

- ❏ 30" access in front of panels
- ❏ Emergency Lighting
- ❏ Illuminated Exit Signs

Restrooms:

- ❑ Number Required:
- ❑ Number Required (Accessible)

Kitchen:

- ❑ Wall Covering
- ❑ Cove Base
- ❑ Flooring
- ❑ Ceiling Type
- ❑ Lighting Type

Equipment:

- ❑ Ware Washing Sink
- ❑ Prep Sink
- ❑ Hand Sink(s)
- ❑ Floor Drains/Sinks
- ❑ Freezer
- ❑ Cooler / Refrigerator
- ❑ Hot Water Heater
- ❑ Grinder
- ❑ Grease Trap
- ❑ Hood
    - -Duct Run
    - -Mechanical Information
- ❑ Additional Equipment

Plumbing:

- ❑ Backflow Prevention Device Note
- ❑ Water Heater

Employee Storage:

Chemical Storage:

Pest Prevention Plan:

Waste Information:

Finishes:

Ceiling:

Wall Material:

Flooring:

Counter:

ACKNOWLEDGEMENTS

Many thanks to God above who makes all things possible.

To all of my amazing clients with Tasty Space Businesses: You have taken on exceptional endeavors and I am impressed by the dedication you display to your craft.

To my awesome team of consultants who are able to make any Tasty Space the best space ever.

To following people who have helped me on this incredible journey to becoming The Foodie Builder:

> To my sister, Patricia Middleton, author, editor, nomenclator, and publishing consultant. Thank you for listening to all of my dreams and helping me develop my brand.

> To my mother, Phyllis Nicholson Middleton, my biggest fan and best supporter: Thank you for always helping me to do what I do and be all that I can be.

> To my brother, Reggie Middleton: Thank you for your help, advice, and listening ear.

Thank you to the contributing authors of this book: Chef Yolanda Lockhart-Davis (Chapter 2), Dr. Renaldo Octavius Epps (Chapter 5), and Environmental Health Specialist Lamar Smith (Chapter 7).

Thank you to Tiffany Gray and Marguerite Anglin for your contributions to the cover design.

Thank you to Robert Rodriguez and the late Robert Mendelsohn for your photographic contributions to this book.

Thank you to A. Robert Torres and Zach Torres of Studio Torres for providing the opportunity for me to work on a few great restaurant projects with you.

Thank you to author, architect and artist, Marguerite Anglin for your creative and professional contributions to the development of The Foodie Builder.

Thank you to Lisa Balthaser of Fleur De Lisa Solutions for your marketing contributions.

Special thanks to Jerome Shabazz of the Overbrook Environmental Arts Center.

And special thanks to Calvin Joshua Crawford, Angel and Shannon Garcia, Cedric Middleton, our film crew and all of my guests on Season 2 of Aesthetically Speaking. You helped contribute information helpful in the process of planning and building food facilities. This season, we will discuss the planning and building of Tasty Spaces.

Jackie Ball, Realtor

Chef Rafyah Lumb, Love Creations

Chef Ashe Reynolds

Chef Yolanda Lockhardt-Davis, Salt Pepper and Soul

Chef Char Nolan

John McClenney, Architect and Contractor, Yes Dear

Chivonne Green-Washington, Interior Designer, CY Interiors

Lamar Smith, Author, Restaurant Owner, Environmental Health Inspector

E. Scot Fields, Financial Planner, Business Consultant, CEO Council

Paul Marrone, Owner, A Tutti Restaurant

This project was truly a collaborative effort including all who have supported and encouraged the development, and progress of The Foodie Builder brand and its projects. To all of you, including clients, business consultants, friends and family, I am eternally grateful. If I have excluded anyone in these acknowledgements, please charge it to my head and not my heart.

ABOUT THE AUTHOR

Felicia Middleton, "The Foodie Builder," is the owner of Urban Aesthetics, a design and planning firm located in Philadelphia.

Felicia began designing restaurants and food facilities 15 years ago with a South Jersey Commercial Kitchen design firm that specialized in designing food facilities, restaurants and bars in Casinos and Schools throughout New Jersey and the United States. While working there, Felicia developed her design and planning skills while learning a new specialty. She worked on several notable projects including a commissary kitchen in Vineland New Jersey; Cafeteria food lines for several Vineland schools and Back of House dish rooms and kitchens for the Foxwoods Casino in Rhode Island.

Since starting her company in 2008, Felicia has worked designing and planning many local restaurants and food areas and facilities, including several restaurants at The Bourse Food Hall, Philadelphia and the following notable restaurants: The Palm; Rosa's Fresh Pizza, 1 and 2 and the Tropical Smoothie Cafe, located on Temple University's campus.

OTHER BOOKS BY FELICIA LISA MIDDLETON

Your PATH to Green: Designing an Eco-Friendly Map for Your Life and Your Space

(2012)

This book is a must read for business leaders, entrepreneurs, designers, and anyone else concerned with having a positive impact on the local or global environment.

Metamorphosis: Aesthetic Poetry

(2013)

Like metamorphic rocks, you may go through circumstances and experiences that cause you to change, however, change is inevitable. Embrace it. Take charge of it. The results can be exciting.

A Complete Guide to Creating Commercial Spaces

(2020)

This textbook will help guide you through the process of opening a Brick and Mortar Business.

NOTES

NOTES

NOTES

A Complete Guide to Creating Tasty Spaces

NOTES

NOTES

NOTES

Made in the USA
Middletown, DE
23 December 2021

56909520R10068